# CAMBRIDGESHIRE & SUFFOLK

Edited By Lawrence Smith

First published in Great Britain in 2018 by:

Young Writers
Remus House
Coltsfoot Drive
Peterborough
PE2 9BF
Telephone: 01733 890066
Website: www.youngwriters.co.uk

All Rights Reserved
Book Design by Ben Reeves
© Copyright Contributors 2018
SB ISBN 978-1-78896-829-4
Printed and bound in the UK by BookPrintingUK
Website: www.bookprintinguk.com
YB0378DZ

# FOREWORD

Young Writers was created in 1991 with the express purpose of promoting and encouraging creative writing. Each competition we create is tailored to the relevant age group, hopefully giving each child the inspiration and incentive to create their own piece of writing, whether it's a poem or a short story. We truly believe that seeing it in print gives pupils a sense of achievement and pride in their work and themselves.

Our latest competition, Monster Poetry, focuses on uncovering the different techniques used in poetry and encouraging pupils to explore new ways to write a poem. Using a mix of imagination, expression and poetic styles, this anthology is an impressive snapshot of the inventive, original and skilful writing of young people today. These poems showcase the creativity and talent of these budding new writers as they learn the skills of writing, and we hope you are as entertained by them as we are.

# CONTENTS

## Independent Entries

| | |
|---|---|
| Catrin Naomi Andrews (9) | 1 |

## Beaumont Primary School, Hadleigh

| | |
|---|---|
| Hayden Earle-Mitchell (10) | 4 |
| Bruno Canha (10) | 5 |
| Thaila Francis Herridge (8) | 6 |
| Brecon Bamsey (10) | 7 |
| Layton Lewis Davies (10) | 8 |
| Sophie Woodman (8) | 9 |
| Bradley Carr (11) | 10 |
| Sophie Henderson (9) | 11 |
| Connor Earle Mitchell (8) | 12 |
| Amy Gardner (7) | 13 |
| Oliver Vince (9) | 14 |
| Ethan Henderson (7) | 15 |
| Carson Patel (9) | 16 |
| Izzy Smith (10) | 17 |
| Chloe Ava Dawes (8) | 18 |
| Madison Millar (8) | 19 |

## Centre Academy East Anglia, Ipswich

| | |
|---|---|
| Taylor David Aaron Tonner (9) | 20 |
| Isabelle Haywood (10) | 21 |
| Edward Alex Theo Scott (11) | 22 |

## Chelmondiston CE (VC) Primary School, Chelmondiston

| | |
|---|---|
| Orla Baines (8) | 23 |
| Anna Weeding (11) | 24 |
| Savannah Rose Irene Davis (8) | 26 |
| Tallula Rose Millett (9) | 28 |
| Marie Jacqueline Patricia Prosser (9) | 29 |
| Holly Wright (9) | 30 |
| Liberty Bell (8) | 31 |
| Charlie Britton (9) | 32 |
| Robert Norman (8) | 33 |
| Bonnie Looe Nicoll (8) | 34 |
| Gracie Armes (8) | 35 |
| Evelyn Iris Alexander (9) | 36 |
| Layla Bones (8) | 37 |
| Willow Bond Carter (10) | 38 |

## Chilton Community Primary School, Stowmarket

| | |
|---|---|
| Mercy Fox (10) | 39 |
| Angel Bussey (9) | 40 |

## Earl Soham Community Primary School, Earl Soham

| | |
|---|---|
| Riley Sadd (8) | 41 |
| Molly Dorsett (9) | 42 |

## Leverington Primary Academy, Leverington

| | |
|---|---|
| Grace Olivia Webb (10) | 43 |

## Over Primary School, Over

| | |
|---|---|
| Tabitha Ashurst (9) | 44 |
| Maisey Jane Greenhow (11) | 47 |
| Daisy Holliday (11) | 48 |
| Jacob Michael John Brown (10) | 50 |
| Anna Miller (11) | 52 |
| Daisy Obi | 54 |
| Sienna Mayo (9) | 56 |
| Samuel Parker (11) | 57 |
| Maxi Ward (10) | 58 |
| Ella Welch (10) | 59 |
| Daisy-May Collett (11) | 60 |
| Luke Jodin (11) | 62 |
| Harriet Cotton (10) | 63 |
| Millie Clark (10) | 64 |
| Dylan Jamie Wadsworth (10) | 65 |
| Coco Shooter (9) | 66 |
| Alex Sturman (10) | 67 |
| Joseph Harris (10) | 68 |
| Will Ford (9) | 69 |
| Noah Nightingale | 70 |
| Caleb Smith (10) | 71 |
| Callum Hillier (10) | 72 |
| Sophie Simpson (11) | 73 |
| Mya Gormer (10) | 74 |
| Amber Fabish (11) | 75 |
| Charlie Harrison (10) | 76 |
| Eleanor Pilsworth (9) | 77 |
| James Crawford (10) | 78 |
| James Day (10) | 79 |
| Fin Websdale (9) | 80 |
| Lola Rosa Oliva (10) | 81 |
| Jack Sheppard (11) | 82 |
| Luke Smith (11) | 83 |

## St Andrew's CE (VC) Primary School, Bulmer

| | |
|---|---|
| Justin Brown (9) | 84 |
| Charlie Mayes-Allen (7) | 86 |
| Louis Emile Josse (9) | 87 |
| Ellie Elizabeth Spencer (9) | 88 |
| Mason Damarackas (9) | 89 |
| Alexander Cox (8) | 90 |
| Logan Pressling (9) | 91 |
| Amy Elizabeth Russell (8) | 92 |
| Alfie Mayes-Allen (9) | 93 |
| George Griffiths (8) | 94 |

## St Philip's CE Primary School, Cambridge

| | |
|---|---|
| Matilda Farrar (8) | 95 |
| Megan Woodward (8) | 96 |
| Otis Hamilton (9) | 98 |
| Emilia Rose Bates (7) | 100 |
| Josh Roth (9) | 102 |
| Finn Beardwell (8) | 103 |
| Kiera Molloy (9) | 104 |
| Connie Cotton | 105 |
| Lilly-Rose Alderson (9) | 106 |
| Ellina Russell (8) | 107 |
| Charleigh McDonnell (9) | 108 |
| Althea Jasmaine Ladia Erum (8) | 109 |
| Tom Dunne (7) | 110 |
| Samuel Unsworth (9) | 111 |
| Mollie Brown (7) | 112 |
| Rhys Brown (8) | 113 |
| Anna Koscielny-Lemaire (9) | 114 |
| Sumayyah H Rahman (9) | 115 |
| Charlotte Skates (8) | 116 |
| Imodgen Hodges (8) | 117 |
| Alma Dunne (9) | 118 |
| Mali Hardinge (7) | 119 |
| Jay Evely (9) | 120 |
| Michael Hudson (8) | 121 |
| Corin McCarthy (8) | 122 |
| Honor Day (7) | 123 |
| Emily Sutton (9) | 124 |

Elliot Glasberg (9) 125
Gideon Wilder Lynn (9) 126

## Waldringfield Primary School, Waldringfield

Leah Davidson (10) 127

## West Walton Community Primary School, West Walton

Alex Edward Clare (11) 128
Holly Pepper (10) 129
Imogen Hopps (11) 130
Rosie Fensom (11) 131
Charlotte Walker (10) 132
Chloe Puttock (10) 133

# THE POEMS

# A Puppy Flew To The Moon

A puppy flew to the moon,
He landed with a *bump!*
Then he heard someone say...
"What was that loud *thump?*"

"It was my rocket,
It's red and it's pink,
It has a big round body,
It even has a sink."

"That's not okay!
It's not okay at all!
My cart is all wrecked!
Now make a call!"

"But to whom?"
The puppy asked.
"Is it a man?"
But then someone just gasped.

"Is it a woman?
Or an ape?

Maybe a tree frog?
Or perhaps a snake?"

"Is it a squirrel?
Or a cat?
Maybe a parrot?
Or perhaps, maybe that?"

A scary, tall figure
appeared behind,
The scared, little dog
who had lost his mind.

"I'd better run
back to my rocket,
Go through the door
and then lock it."

He flew down to Earth,
He ran to his home,
And his owner said...
"Were you alone?"

"Time for tea,
Come on boy, sit down,
I'll get your bowl,
Little Bernard Brown."

## Catrin Naomi Andrews (9)

# Bulbasaur

In the mountains there arose a sound
When something appeared shaking the ground
A shape appeared
As the rocks revolved into place
I suddenly saw a ranting face
The unnerving beast was formed from rock
Its diminutive, menacing eyes
Were as green as freshly polished emeralds
His boulder-strewn body was extremely Herculean
With his bulky, murderous fingers
He crushed people in an instant
Its bulbous body was excessively abundant
Meaning its every step formed an
immense earthquake
Seizing his prey wasn't easy
But when he caught it he would rip it up
limb from limb
Using his blunt, extensive teeth
Bulbasaur preyed on humans
Especially the obese ones.

### Hayden Earle-Mitchell (10)
Beaumont Primary School, Hadleigh

# The Inferno Hound

Rumbling from the volcano the monster burst out,
Shooting sparks of scorching fire,
His blazing red eyes causing fear to anyone
he looks at,
Gnashing his gleaming teeth made of molten lava,
He stopped anything in his terror-filled path,
His razor-sharp claws would burn everything
they touched,
When hitting the ground volcanoes would erupt,
He dashed around like a cheetah,
He darted as fast as lightning,
Devoured his prey by burning through their necks,
Then used his teeth just to check,
He had cracks all around his body,
Showing bits of molten lava,
It was said he was born in a volcano
And he lives in the magma under the crust.

## Bruno Canha (10)
Beaumont Primary School, Hadleigh

# Max The Monster

I met a monster at a race,
We had fun all day!
Soon he said, "My name is Max!"
We ate our tea until it was three!
Though didn't I notice he gave me a bonus,
But once he turned evil! A real baddie!
He slimed the house with a big shovel.
"This place is a disgrace!"
But nobody knew he was still a friend,
When he saw me he gave me a hug!
We entered our race!
As the sun turned to me,
We had a great time that day!
We went on a Ferris wheel going in a circle!
Onto a roundabout, off all those races!
Growing up with Max is a struggle,
As he is a bubble!

## Thaila Francis Herridge (8)
Beaumont Primary School, Hadleigh

# The Deviate

Riding in the wind like the mist of a tornado,
Spreading its wings that brightly glow,
Scanning the area his intense eyes darted around,
As swiftly and silently it swooped to the ground,
Swishing and swaying his razor-sharp tail,
Everything tumbled and fell from his trail,
Gliding silently across the sky,
All that was heard was a little whispering voice,
Using his beak he hunts his prey,
Then stabbing it eagerly to death,
He munched with joy,
Devouring it in seconds,
The malevolent beast was satisfied.

**Brecon Bamsey (10)**
Beaumont Primary School, Hadleigh

# The Unsuspected Thing...

Erupting from a volcano came,
A molten beast so murderous and mean,
Leaping onto the earth,
With an immense *bang!*
With his malicious red staring eyes,
He stares into the soul of every person who looked at him,
When he takes the souls of people,
He devours them in less than three seconds,
He is as black as death and has red dots
And spikes as hot and red as lava,
He moves as swiftly as water flowing
And as smoothly as a dolphin soaring through the sea.

## Layton Lewis Davies (10)
Beaumont Primary School, Hadleigh

# Fizzy's Secret Poem

*Gobble, gobble, munch, munch,*
Fizzy loves a good munch.
He loves to eat, he loves to play,
He'll cuddle anyone for the day!

Fizzy's furry and blue
And if he sees a person then he'll get them,
He might even come after you!

*Gobble, gobble, crunch, crunch,*
Fizzy loves a good munch.
The hat he wears is black and blue,
Although Fizzy is friendly,
He will chase you.

What would you do if a monster came for you?

## Sophie Woodman (8)
Beaumont Primary School, Hadleigh

# The Feathered Beast

Emerging from a stormy cloud
A feathered beast appeared
Its beak like a mouth
Began to shriek aloud

Its eyes were darting everywhere
Penetrating like a knife
Whoever looked straight into them
Had to run for their sorry little life

When the beast moves
It spins around rapidly
Then eventually darts around
To reach its prey

When it eats,
It savagely devours gigantic animals
And, on rare occasions, defenceless humans.

**Bradley Carr (11)**
Beaumont Primary School, Hadleigh

# Happy Healing Monster

Happy, weird healing monster,
In a cave being brave,
Grinning cheekily,
Two blushing cheeks,
One eye higher,
Other lower.

Happy, weird healing monster,
With his big, beady eyes,
Watching he glares,
At all the people,
That pass by in the streets
And greets everyone he meets.

Would you be friends
With the Happy Healing Monster?

**Sophie Henderson (9)**
Beaumont Primary School, Hadleigh

# Rob's Secret Poem

Hi my name is Rob
I like corn on the cob
My friend is Bob
People call me names like 'rubbish Rob'
I turn invisible when I'm in danger
I'm a friend, not a foe
I am a foot tall
I'm going to a Royal Ball
Sweden is my favourite place
My pet is a pug
I've got two bug suckers on each side.

## Connor Earle Mitchell (8)
Beaumont Primary School, Hadleigh

# Leo's Story

In a deep, dark forest
Zoomed a monster
Leo was his name
Smartest monster in the world
Camouflage monster
Hungry monster
Hungriest monster in the world
Living in a dangerous cave
Looking like a turtle
Hiding between the dark grey rocks
Waiting for a panda bear to approach.

**Amy Gardner (7)**
Beaumont Primary School, Hadleigh

# Scary Fred!

I am Fred,
I sit on the rusty roof,
I watch you all the time!
Run, run, run,
I am coming
For you!
I am evil,
I will pick you up
And eat you.
I will drown you
In bogeys and snot.
I am angry,
I have no friends,
No family,
*Wah! Wah! Wah!*

## Oliver Vince (9)
Beaumont Primary School, Hadleigh

# The Greedy Grinch!

Wild, fierce, green and hairy
Three-toed, green-headed monster
Living in a cave
Has no friends
Called a Grinch
Greedy for passers-by
Fluffy but aggressive
Waiting for someone to pass by
Opens his tiny mouth to make it huge
Gobbles all that pass.

## Ethan Henderson (7)
Beaumont Primary School, Hadleigh

# Zig-Zag

Wicked wild monster waiting for someone.
One red eye,
One googly pink eye!
Big and as strong as an ox.
Up high on the crimson, sparkling roof.
Snacking on people,
*Gobble, gobble, munch, munch,*
*Crunch, crunch, crunch!*

## Carson Patel (9)
Beaumont Primary School, Hadleigh

# Ice Monster

Breaking out of the glassy ice barn
Scraping and lashing with its terrible claws
The creature cracked out in no time at all
Bright yellow glowing eyes glared
Sharp, pointy spikes creeping up his back
They are as sharp as a knife.

**Izzy Smith (10)**
Beaumont Primary School, Hadleigh

# Adorable Monster Rainbow

Smiling with delight
Two teeth at the top
And the others at the bottom
Fuzzy, hilarious and light as a feather
Waiting, watching
Standing on her blue balcony
Waiting for her friend to arrive
*Roar! Roar! Roar!*

## Chloe Ava Dawes (8)
Beaumont Primary School, Hadleigh

# George's Favourite Poem

Major monster
Loves the purple colour
Likes sneakers
Giant monster
Ugly but nice
Fun to play with
Sad, lonely, crying
When he has no one to play with.

## Madison Millar (8)
Beaumont Primary School, Hadleigh

# Monstania

M ontsania is a gigantic and gentle monster
O nly coming out at night when the kids go home
N aughty things happen when he's about
S tinky breath comes from his mouth with rotten fangs
T alons and tongue as long as a pencil
A lways stomping around and looking scary with eyes like laser beams
N ever being mean to anyone
I t is all about the love he gives
A nd the great big gentle hugs too.

**Taylor David Aaron Tonner (9)**
Centre Academy East Anglia, Ipswich

# The Robob

Watch out all kids
As the Robob is coming
He hides in shadows and underground
All he ever eats is children
For breakfast, dinner and lunch
He loves them and thinks they're scrummy
Especially on toast
He never eats adults though
He says they taste like worms.

## Isabelle Haywood (10)
Centre Academy East Anglia, Ipswich

# Aargh!

The name is Twinkle Dead
I am a dragon
With ten eyes and ten wings
I have ten heads
My claws are really sharp
I have horns on all my heads
Everyone runs from me in fear
But I don't care
It's because of my underwear.

## Edward Alex Theo Scott (11)
Centre Academy East Anglia, Ipswich

# Squiggly-Bubble Causes Trouble

My monster, Squiggly-Bubble
Has lots of stubble
And he's always getting in trouble.
I found him one day in the bin,
While I was putting some rubbish in,
He popped up and said, "Please be my friend,"
Now he's driving me round the bend.
I went home, he followed me round,
He hardly ever makes a sound,
Except when my friends come round to play,
Then he acts in a very different way.
He may look as sweet as a daisy,
But actually, he's really crazy!
He stamps muddy footprints onto the floor
And bangs his head upon the door.
That's why I'm telling you,
Never speak to a Squiggly-Bubble
Otherwise, it'll cause you trouble!

### Orla Baines (8)
Chelmondiston CE (VC) Primary School, Chelmondiston

# Montaigous The Monster

I opened my door and guess who I saw
Montaigous the monster that's what I saw
He opened his mouth as if to talk
But all he could do was grunt and snort
He gestured to the sea upon the north
And hurried away on his stubby little toes
I ran after him following his candyfloss-like hair
As the green blob in the distance
That was Montaigous
Got fainter and fainter
I questioned my healthiness
Out of breath and the wind in my hair
I finally stopped and saw where I was, the beach
The beach, the best place of all
What I saw was the worst of all
"Montaigous, Montaigous!" I called
As he jumped into the sea and sailed away
Sailing and paddling harder and harder
The further he went the more faint he became
The once bright green blob that was his body
Had become a black matchstick figure

Into the fog that was covering the sea
He was truly gone.

## Anna Weeding (11)
Chelmondiston CE (VC) Primary School, Chelmondiston

# Pom Of The Pompom World

Pom was a queen,
The very best there's been,
She was fluffy,
She was puffy,
Doesn't matter, she was cute.

Pom lived in a castle,
A very tall castle,
It had walls and doors,
Four floors and ten stairs,
It was huge.

Pom had knights,
That went out at night,
Flying a kite,
They rode to the town,
They rode down.

Pom eats grapes,
She recorded lots of tapes,
The knights ate dates.

Pom drinks grape juice,
Knights drink moose blood.

Her pet was a Pomeranian,
She rode her horse, Lily,
She had a gold crown
And wore a gold gown,
Pom... Is... Great!

## Savannah Rose Irene Davis (8)
Chelmondiston CE (VC) Primary School, Chelmondiston

# Born Out Of A Nightmare

Born out of a night scream,
This monster was the opposite to a
goodnight dream,
Her teeth were razors and her eyes shot lasers.
She was always hungry and in need of feeding,
If you don't feed her it would be you bleeding.
All ends well but keep one eye open tonight,
Or you'll be the one screaming in fright.
Pimples of pus, do not fuss,
For she is red all over with scales of stuff.
She did, however, have a soft spot in her heart
And if you lifted your leg she would
laugh and giggle,
At the sound of your fart.
I warn you don't have a good night's dream,
Or she'll be after you!
Beware!

## Tallula Rose Millett (9)
Chelmondiston CE (VC) Primary School, Chelmondiston

# All Alone

You lie in your bed,
Not a whisper to be said,
You close your eyes
And a shadow leaps behind you!
You sit up and a face right there,
Staring at you,
Their eyes glowing
And a murderous heart is in sight.
"Is it a dream?" you say out loud.
"No!" the demon replies boldly.
You cry and cry with fear crawling up your spine.
"It's okay! I didn't mean to scare you."
Your face beams with relief,
"Okay, but leave for I am trying to sleep."
Your heart fills up with grief for you're
alone once more,
He leaves with a puff and *pfft!*

## Marie Jacqueline Patricia Prosser (9)
Chelmondiston CE (VC) Primary School, Chelmondiston

# Naughty Nugget

Cute on the outside, mean on the inside,
He's part of an evil gang,
Tricks people very easily with his cute, shiny eyes
And his high-pitched voice,
You can barely hear.

If you say a mean comment,
He can backchat back,
Even though you wouldn't think it,
For his bright blue, fluffy coat,
You surely would not expect such a surprise.

He's really, really tiny
And you can also see,
His bones the slightest bit,
He has duck feet and two different types of hand,
Bear ears and diamond eyes, he ought to be a pet.

**Holly Wright (9)**
Chelmondiston CE (VC) Primary School, Chelmondiston

# I Have Big Fangs

I'm a monster as big as can be
As wild as a lion
As mythical as a mermaid (but not as nice!)
Watch me bite
Watch me growl
I have big, fat fangs
I have eight fingers
Four legs, four toes, two arms
My eyes are green
I love to scream
I only come out at night in your dreams
Dream good things or I will come to life
I eat meat and drink blood!
I love my appetite
I hide in your wardrobe
Eat you at night
And that's my appetite
Watch out kids, here I come!
What am I?

A vampire!

## Liberty Bell (8)
Chelmondiston CE (VC) Primary School, Chelmondiston

# Heroicness Of Yetizard

Once there was a monster called Yetizard
He is hairy, terrifying and weird
His fur feels like 1,000 feathers
His claws are sharp as his horns

He has a friend called Freezion
They both live in a place called Antizon
It was cold and snowy

One fateful day he went to Earth
There was a fire
With the heat it made a big choir
All of the monsters tramping go through the flames
As Yetizard was scared he called Freezion
Who used his freeze breath to freeze the fire.

## Charlie Britton (9)
Chelmondiston CE (VC) Primary School, Chelmondiston

# Smelly!

Oh! Smelly you naughty boy,
Ooh Smelly where did you go,
Oh Smelly what did I tell you?
Don't go crushing planets!

Oh! Smelly don't be rude,
Ooh Smelly what have you done?
Oh Smelly get away,
You're in your bedroom for the day.

So Smelly is ten times the size of the sun,
Smelly is a planet-crushing alien,
He was born by the universe,
Out comes smelly in a strop,
He shut the door madly,
Smelly just passed quite sadly!

## Robert Norman (8)
Chelmondiston CE (VC) Primary School, Chelmondiston

# Music Monster

May I introduce myself to you,
My name is Music Monster, achoo!
Sorry, I'm a sneezy thing,
But I love to dab, floss and sing.
I sing when I'm happy, I sing when I'm sad,
But I am a monster so don't make me mad!
My head is big, my feet are small,
My fangs are sharp, I'm really cool!
So if you think you could be like me,
Or even think that possibly,
You are different in any way,
Sing loud, sing proud and be a Music Monster every day.

## Bonnie Looe Nicoll (8)
Chelmondiston CE (VC) Primary School, Chelmondiston

# The Glider

I swoop in the sky with only two eyes
My fur as dark as the midnight skies
I glide with glee, swooping into the stellar sky
I look around and don't hear a sound
But you're the only thing around
The trees towering before me
But you're the only thing flying before me
*Hoot*, says the owl full of thoughts
*Moo*, goes the cow miraculously
But there are many other creatures around.

## Gracie Armes (8)
Chelmondiston CE (VC) Primary School, Chelmondiston

# Vile Pernicious

His name is Vile Pernicious,
He lives in your mind.
He's ugly and mean.
When you wake up he'll be there,
Crossing his five legs.
He looks between your eyes,
Watching your every move.
He'll make you disappear in worry.
He'll never stop being mean.
No! That's his thing, being mean.
So when you wake up be sure to know,
You've got a devil inside you!
Mwahahaha!

## Evelyn Iris Alexander (9)
Chelmondiston CE (VC) Primary School, Chelmondiston

# Soaring Swiftly

Soaring swiftly above the sky
What is that I spy with my little eye?
Small and fluffy with elegant rainbow wings
I hear its voice so loud it sings
Upon its head I see a flash
It's scared me now so off I dash
I sit and watch, quiet as a mouse
Its talons are as sharp as a shard of glass
I see a smile upon its face
Maybe she wants to be friends
Not all monsters are bad you know.

## Layla Bones (8)
Chelmondiston CE (VC) Primary School, Chelmondiston

# Fluffy Menace

Stomping through the town
Terrorising crowds
Creeping into pet shops
Eating all the cats and dogs
No more hamsters and bunnies
Not a single budgie left
Scared I'm next
He is coming towards me
Throwing him a teddy bear
Him looking quite surprised
Tears came to his eyes
He did not want to terrorise
"Sorry," he said, "want to get some fries?"

**Willow Bond Carter (10)**
Chelmondiston CE (VC) Primary School, Chelmondiston

# The Cheeky Monster

The cheeky monster lived alone,
Even though he was cheeky,
He had a naughty devil that lived in his horns
And when the monster was sad he would cuddle people.
People thought he was ugly but it's because he's a monster
And no one hugged him except his BFF.
They call him 'TM' because he's a troublemaker!
If I saw the monster I would give him a hug
And then I would go home to bed.
Every night I would think about him,
He would be like a brother to me.

## Mercy Fox (10)
Chilton Community Primary School, Stowmarket

# The Trip To Earth

Clump is a wild thing
No one knows how he's like that
Clever Clump, nails as sharp as knives
Can cut anything you like
But friendly as a banana peel
Clump all alone in the middle of spacious space
Good Clump, get to Earth
Clump turned invisible instantly
Then he fell in a volcano and lost his invisibility
After he met a girl
The girl kept Clump in a plastic pot
Clump was joyful as a monster could be
After three years Clump returned home,
back to Mars!

## Angel Bussey (9)
Chilton Community Primary School, Stowmarket

# Noscoper 360

My name is Noscoper 360
I have eyes all red and wild
My claws are as sharp as a needle
For those never get filed.

I have big wavy ears that flap in people's faces
And sharp pointy teeth
That sparkle like silver space places.

My tummy is wobbly like jelly
And my legs are all slimy and scaly
I have hands with small dangly fingers
That walk along being all feely.

My colour is yellow, I don't like it much
It is disgusting, sickly to touch
I want to turn gooey green
So please colour me or I'll scream.

## Riley Sadd (8)
Earl Soham Community Primary School, Earl Soham

# Cute Creep

A kingdom crusher
A human musher
As scary as a shark
She hides in the midnight dark
Humans go hiding
While she is still busily finding
Those people who didn't hide had a sight
Now they are in a stew for tonight
Though she may sound ugly
She looks so cute and cuddly
But don't be fooled by her eyes
Or you will be in for a nasty surprise!
Wings as beautiful as a butterfly
Hair rainbow bright
Camouflaged in darkness
She'll definitely give you a fright!

**Molly Dorsett (9)**
Earl Soham Community Primary School, Earl Soham

# Meddling Monsters

This is rebellious Ramani,
He is from the planet Vast Venus,
He has two frightening friends:
Raw Raw and Sulana.
He is the worst of the worst.

Ruffleclaw lives in a cold crater,
He is 888 years old
And he is the meanest monster,
On his perfect planet.

### Grace Olivia Webb (10)
Leverington Primary Academy, Leverington

# Realisation

Creeping cautiously down the hallway,
It's very late at night,
Looking round each corner,
There's nobody in sight.

Until I see a light shining,
From an open door,
I peer my heavy head around
And spy a little girl of four.

Her bright eyes sparkled,
With happy thoughts in her head,
Carefree and oblivious,
On her pink, fluffy bed.

That bed looked soft and comfy,
Those teddies cute and cuddly,
I longed to join in all the fun,
But then suddenly...

Her eyes caught mine through the door crack,
Teddy fell and she backed away,

Her smile disappeared from her sweet face,
I'm guessing she didn't want to play.

She screamed the loudest I'd ever heard,
I nearly fell over in fright,
Frantically calling for her mum,
And behind me clicked on a light.

I sprinted down the empty hallway,
Searching for somewhere to hide,
I found a door and slipped through it quick,
I've never been so petrified.

But I chose the room unwisely,
For there in front of me,
Stood a hideous beast with big sharp teeth,
Looking at me wildly.

He was staring terrified and trembling,
Directly into my eyes,
He looked just as afraid as I was of him,
So imagine my surprise.

When I stuttered the words "W... Who are you?"
His mouth moved in time,

It occurred to me that it was a mirror,
The reflection *was mine!*

## Tabitha Ashurst (9)
Over Primary School, Over

# The Terrorbee!

If you close your door,
Get onto the floor,
Lower your head
And gaze under your bed,
For what will be there,
Will give you a scare,
For you will see,
The Terrorbee!

"What is a Terrorbee?" I hear you ask,
Is it your sister wearing a mask?
No it's a monster! With wide-open jaws,
Scary red eyes
And sharp serrated claws.
"What does it eat?" You must be thinking,
Well, it only eats socks that are rather stinking.

If you don't want this monster under your bed,
Think very carefully and use your head,
Pick up your socks
And tidy them away,
Be sure to do this each and every day!

## Maisey Jane Greenhow (11)
Over Primary School, Over

# I Did Warn You!

Have you ever heard about evil Lord Parlic,
He acts so much like a Dalek,
His favourite sound is hearing blood splatter
And I think this is an important matter...

His scales are as blue as the deep blue sea,
He also has invisibility,
Six sticky limbs mean he can climb,
He also vomits up the grossest slime...

He shoots heinous laser beams from
his scarlet eyes,
Which definitely gives people a nasty surprise,
A grotesque scare runs down his face,
He also carries a spotty briefcase...

Inside the briefcase of unknown
Is, of course, an emergency phone,
Which can do something that'll make you queer,
The thing is to destroy the atmosphere...

A lava gun that can burn you in no time at all,
But that is not all that can break a wall

I won't go into the gory details,
I'll move onto his horrific toenails...

Needle-like talons rip up the soil,
So he doesn't slip over in the slippiest of oil,
He can *crunch* bones with his monster claws,
Yet don't get me started on his dreadful jaws...

I think I've said enough to give you a nightmare,
And make your everything shiver, even your hair,
He lurks in the blue,
I did warn you...
*I did warn you!*

## Daisy Holliday (11)
Over Primary School, Over

# Grumpy Stumpy

Stumpy was his name
Being grumpy was his game
With beady eyes and root-like legs
And smelly fur just like rotten eggs
He lived alone inside a tree
He was lonely as could be
Stumpy wanted a loyal friend
Who cared not, should his smell offend.

One day the blackest raven came to say his hello
His squawking woke the inhabitants of the enchanted forest below
Stumpy flew into a rage and trapped the noisy bird inside a cage
The days went by and Stumpy began to feel regret
How could he imprison this bird, he was wild not a pet!

Stumpy released the bird into the sky
But the raven came back - can you guess why?
That's right - the raven saw Stumpy as his friend
Someone upon whom he could depend.

The lesson to my tale is clear
Be happy not grumpy
Be kind not mean
You will make the truest friends this way
Just like old Stumpy!

**Jacob Michael John Brown (10)**
Over Primary School, Over

# This Is Just A Hairy Monster Poem

This is just a hairy monster poem
No ghouls, no ghosts, no spiders and no worms
It might not sound like one but wait until
it gets going
Just wait until you meet Mary, she's
very easy-going
In fact, let me introduce you guys to her!

This is Mary
She's ever so hairy
Even lonely
Monsters at Hair Hill School call her 'mildew
mouth' or 'monster mat'
As I said she's very easy-going so she pulled out
her pet rat
She explained her difference and her bullies
without a teardrop
The rat instantly replied with, "Never
listen to them,
Just own what they make fun of you for."

With these words, hairy Mary skipped down the hall
With lingering puffs of stink smoke.

## Anna Miller (11)
Over Primary School, Over

# This Monster Is Not A Monster

Deep beneath the marine blue ocean,
Lives a creature in an underwater cave.
*Splash! Splash!* Each day it will swim towards what shone
And sit under the molten-hot sun.
There it will show off its mint green spikes on its back
And plum purple pebble eyes,
That dazzle in the sun.
But this monster is not a monster!

Embedded in the rose gold sand,
It will sing an obnoxious melody,
As if a frog was stuck in its throat.
There along with the appalling singing,
It will jump so heavily that it wakes up the dead.
But this monster is *not* a monster!
This monster is a human that was born not to blend in

But to stand out.
This monster is not a monster.

## Daisy Obi
Over Primary School, Over

# Smiley!

Smiley is kind, caring, thoughtful and nice,
she is as sweet as candyfloss.
Smiley lives in Monsterland.
She is as spotty as a Dalmatian,
Purple, fuzzy hair everywhere,
Shiny white teeth glow in the moonlight,
Smiley eats strawberries dipped in chocolate every night,
Sometimes her hair gets sticky from all the sweets she eats,
Her monster mummy worries that she's having too many treats,
Smiley's emerald eyes shine bright like the stars at night,
Her smile is so big she gives people a fright in case she bites.
When she sits in the dentist's chair the ends of her hair touch the floor.

## Sienna Mayo (9)
Over Primary School, Over

# The Cake Crook

Silently Cake Crook spots his next target
With a spring in his step
And a rumbly, wobbly tummy
He squeezes through the narrow letterbox
Landing swiftly on his padded feet
A faint rumbling of snoring can be
heard from upstairs
Like skyscrapers, his antennae look
Above the kitchen surfaces to locate the cake
Greedy gobbling up gooey cake
Cake Crook makes his escape
As the sun appears off over the horizon
Cheerful chirps greet Cake Monster
As he shares a few crumbs with his
feathered friends
Shrieks are heard as the distraught monster
Discovers the Cake Crook has struck again.

## Samuel Parker (11)
Over Primary School, Over

# Monster Makes A Friend

**M** onster isn't very nice, he has no friends except for his hens.

**O** nce he made a cake with poison and gave it to his teacher Mr Moyson.

**N** o one likes him as he was so mean and the other monsters made fun of his wrinkles and always offered him cream!

**S** ome days because he had no friends he would just go home and sit by his hens.

**T** hen one day he had a brainwave, he needed a friend and he found one called Dave.

**E** very day he would bake him cakes and forever they were best mates.

**R** ealising it was so nice to have a friend he was nice forever and that is the end.

## Maxi Ward (10)
Over Primary School, Over

# Stinky Cyclops

There was a stinky Cyclops that lived down a well,
He washed in dirty water because he loved the smell.
He had no proper food, which put him in a mood,
He dreamt of lovely honey,
But all he got was money.
He was so overweight,
He tried to limit what he ate.
The Cyclops was so lonely,
He had to change his ways,
He needed to find some friends,
To have some happy days,
He left his well, cleaned up his smell,
To try and find some friends,
His search was quick,
In just a click he found them.

## Ella Welch (10)
Over Primary School, Over

# I Know A Monster!

I know a monster,
From Monserat,
With yellow teeth
And a purple hat.

He smells like trash,
His breath is vile,
But his eyes light up,
When he gives a smile.

His skin is hairy,
With feet like cheese,
He is quite scary,
But he likes to please.

His claws are curly
And disgustingly black,
With long skinny arms,
He can scratch his back.

A wart is growing,
At the end of his nose,

But on top of his hat,
He wears a red rose.

## Daisy-May Collett (11)
Over Primary School, Over

# Monster Understood

Once there was a monster,
As ugly as can be,
As scary as a werewolf
And as grumpy as a beast.

Once there was a monster,
Who scared children in their dreams,
He was the stuff of nightmares
And no one dared to see…

This scary five-eyed monster,
As ugly as can be,
Was really very kind inside
And sad no one could see,
No one understood his kind and gentle soul,
Ugly on the outside,
With a heart of gold.

**Luke Jodin (11)**
Over Primary School, Over

# Fluffle Puffle

Fluffle Puffle is a monster,
The meanest one around,
Apart from all her beautiful puffs of rainbow fluff,
She'll attack faster than a bullet,
Until she's had enough.

Puffed up in a ball,
Mewing like a kitten,
Waiting for admirers...

*Boom!* Silver eyes stalking the night,
Like a wolf waiting to fight.
Gleaming horn, ball of fluff,
Dances with jelly beans,
Gosh, she's tough!

## Harriet Cotton (10)
Over Primary School, Over

# My Monster

When I go to bed, I close my eyes tight.
My monster friend whose name is Fred is very big,
With yellow eyes and green ears comes to see me,
There is no light so my monster holds me tight.
I thought it would be scary with my eyes bleary,
But I find it fun because of the things
we have done.
So when morning has come and our
adventure is done,
I open my eyes then realise it was...
It was another bedtime adventure.

## Millie Clark (10)
Over Primary School, Over

# This Is My Monster

This is my monster,
You know the one under the bed,
He is dark green in colour,
With great big orange spots,
He has eight tiny legs
And he is always hungry,
He only wakes at midnight,
So keep your eyes shut
And go to sleep,
He does bite but don't be too frightened,
His teeth aren't used to scare,
He doesn't like to eat you or me,
He'd rather sit and chat
And eat his Weetabix!

## Dylan Jamie Wadsworth (10)
Over Primary School, Over

# Wacky Dacky

My name is Dacky,
I'm sometimes wacky,
I live in a hole,
Just like a mole,
Deep under the ground,
I'm waiting to be found,
I'm ready for tea,
But first a swim in the sea,
Blue and green fishes,
That are giving me wishes,
For tea I have worms,
I love it when they squirm,
Time to go to sleep,
Let's all count some sheep.

## Coco Shooter (9)
Over Primary School, Over

# My Little Monster

My little monster is very cheeky
My small monster is extremely fun
My tiny monster is phenomenally exuberant
My minute monster could be just like you
My mini monster is fabulously clever
My little monster is the best!
My little monster is emerald, azure, rose pink and yellow
My little monster has one massive eye
My little monster is just perfect!

## Alex Sturman (10)
Over Primary School, Over

# Bash!

Bash is young but will get older,
Fluffy he is, it keeps him warm,
In the winter he will get colder.
As Bash is so magical he tells the truth,
"One big, sharp one," he calls his front tooth.
Bash's coat is a carpet of fluff,
So very soft not at all rough,
Yet so friendly he is, he will get tough,
Bash!

## Joseph Harris (10)
Over Primary School, Over

# Medusa

**M** edusa's pride is looking into her enemies' eyes.
**E** yes so cold that they turn you to stone.
**D** are you enter her lair...
**U** nder her spell victims fell.
**S** nakes as hair hiss, curl and turn on top of her head.
**A** hero, a demigod, Perseus slew her with one strike.

## Will Ford (9)
Over Primary School, Over

# Noah The Nice Monster

**M** onsters are mean and horrible,
**O** nly one survives that isn't,
**N** oah is my monster and
**S** ome others think he's loopy,
**T** wo members of his family,
**E** at human eyes to maintain
**R** ed skin for beauty (even though they're ugly)!

## Noah Nightingale
Over Primary School, Over

# The Shongololo Came Creeping

The Shongololo came creeping, creeping,
Hiding in the shadows...
His prey was frightened and weeping,
The Shongololo slithered into the meadow,
The prey, with eyes wide open ran,
As fast as it could into the saucepan!
The Shongololo's mate licked his lips and ate.

## Caleb Smith (10)
Over Primary School, Over

# Bad Monster!

Monsters are mad,
Monsters are bad,
We are glad,
They don't exist.

Monsters are sad today...
Creatures wonder how they are so bad?

The universe is quiet, wait,
The world is still spinning,
The monsters hope for good
And a good mood...

## Callum Hillier (10)
Over Primary School, Over

# Magical Monsters

**M** onsters come out,
**O** n a night like tonight,
**N** ot knowing what is out there,
**S** caring adults,
**T** errifying children,
**E** veryone beware the monsters,
**R** unning around outside,
**S** aying trick or treat everywhere.

## Sophie Simpson (11)
Over Primary School, Over

# Me Monster

It ate its pudding in a delicate way,
Its eyes turned red at the end of the day.
Its intent was fixed and attitude stubborn.
Its revenge was plotted and came all of a sudden.
You will never cross this monster you see,
I know, because this monster is me!

## Mya Gormer (10)
Over Primary School, Over

# Bob The Orange Monster

My name is Bob and I live in a volcano,
I have five blue eyes and orange skin
And smelly yellow teeth like crocodile teeth,
Bob the orange monster, grizzly and hairy,
Like a big, brown bear with sharp claws,
Pointier and pointier as they go on.

**Amber Fabish (11)**
Over Primary School, Over

# Different Monster

This is no ordinary monster,
He didn't have his sharp claws,
He had a nice tone,
He was never light,
People thought he was scary,
Because he was eight foot tall,
But he was friendly,
So this is why he's changed...

## Charlie Harrison (10)
Over Primary School, Over

# Monsters Fun And Games

Monsters are good, monsters are bad,
Monsters are fun,
But monsters can be sad,
My monster is fun
And we like to play our favourite game every day,
I count to ten and he hides,
Once I've found him we swap sides!

## Eleanor Pilsworth (9)
Over Primary School, Over

# Monster

M an-eater, slime-dribbling beast
O nly one of its kind
N obody goes near the beast
S laughtering its prey
T he talons are knives
E verybody who sees it
R un, run away fast!

**James Crawford (10)**
Over Primary School, Over

# Monster Poem

**M** enacing look
**O** greish appearance
**N** asty breath that could make a man die with one blow
**S** caly, horrific skin
**T** he ruby-red eyes
**E** xcruciating bite
**R** aging attitude.

## James Day (10)
Over Primary School, Over

# Drax The Destroyer

**M** ighty meat-eating savage
**O** n the brink of extinction
**N** ightmare inducing
**S** hockingly spiteful
**T** errorises all he encounters
**E** xcruciating sting
**R** azor-sharp teeth.

## Fin Websdale (9)
Over Primary School, Over

# Beady Eyes

Little smile and beady eyes,
When I look up to the sky.
A jelly body jiggling about,
Creepy giggling all about.
Where should I go?
Where should I hide?
It's coming! Aargh!

## Lola Rosa Oliva (10)
Over Primary School, Over

# Loshone

Loshone the horrible monster
Robs from rich monsters
He has a friend called Robo
He lives in a big cave
But Robo is unlike Loshone
Who rages most of the time.

## Jack Sheppard (11)
Over Primary School, Over

# Ill Monster's Atomic Vomit

There once was a monster called Luke,
Who swallowed a military nuke,
His belly was bothered
And then he was smothered,
In radioactive puke.

**Luke Smith (11)**
Over Primary School, Over

# It Is Time For Lunch

*Pop, pop, pop*
*Crunch, crunch, crunch*
I went to get some popcorn with my lunch
Then the packet started to move

I opened the packet
A bit of puffy popcorn came out
I really did doubt
It sucked up some of my popcorn

It got bigger
It looked like a human figure
He was as big as the Titanic
Then I got in a panic

He is not vicious
He is just delicious
I saw his sharp teeth
They smell like roast beef

Then he spoke
He gave me a poke

I was not dreaming
So you should be leaving

He went to head to toe
Then he threw me in the show
Now he is my foe
The popcorn thief that smells like roast beef!

## Justin Brown (9)
St Andrew's CE (VC) Primary School, Bulmer

# Fruit Time Monster

Fruit, fruit, yippee,
Oh no, it's a monster!
Ginormous and strong coming after me!
His head is a green apple,
One arm's a long, yellow corn on the cob,
The other a hard-cooked mushroom,
Tiny baguettes for legs.
*Crunch, crunch, crunch!*
Tiny green peas for eyes,
*Pop! Pop! Pop!*
I scream as he crashes towards me!
I feel a mushroom on my back,
Oh no, I need to get to the track,
As quick as a flash,
A car zoomed by
And splattered his eyes.
As quick as a flash,
I ran to the trash!

## Charlie Mayes-Allen (7)
St Andrew's CE (VC) Primary School, Bulmer

# Chocolate Monster

Chocolate Monster, taller than your door
You better be sure
He breaks your floor
So much chocolate opens your jaw
Marshmallow teeth better than beef
Eyes are oranges, can't be thieved
Strawberry laces for his tongue, how much fun
Don't touch his chocolate feet
They're very deep
He doesn't like his Jeep
But loves his feet
His breath smells like onions
And definitely doesn't have bunions
He was sent to the dungeon
Being alone, no phone
How lonely must he be
Probably eating his teeth.

**Louis Emile Josse (9)**
St Andrew's CE (VC) Primary School, Bulmer

# Melon Monster

Shooting melon at the mouths of men,
Who are all named Len.
Starts off smaller than an ant,
Ends up giant.
Melon fingers reached out to me,
At first I thought it wanted me for tea.
It is as green as grass
And as heavy as brass.
Its surface is smooth,
It doesn't like to have a groove.
*Slurp, slurp, slurp,*
It can't burp.
On the inside as red as a rose,
It has a green nose.
It ends up as my friend,
In the end.

## Ellie Elizabeth Spencer (9)
St Andrew's CE (VC) Primary School, Bulmer

# Chilli Monster

*Crunch, crunch, crunch!*
Hear the monster trudge,
If you make him mad he'll punch,
If you make him punch, he won't eat his lunch.

His head is a sharp pineapple, his eyes are grapes,
His teeth are carrots covered in blood,
He was born in a volcano,
Be careful he could eat you!
If you touch he will melt your skin.
*Slosh, slosh, slosh!*

## Mason Damarackas (9)
St Andrew's CE (VC) Primary School, Bulmer

# Frutti Tutti Monster Man

Its ribs are made out of celery
Its heart is a tomato
The head is a watermelon
The mouth is so big like a pig
It is round and fat like a bat
It can eat a cat on a mat
Its eyes are as red as cherries
It looks like berries
The crusty hands reach out for me
With gross, slimy, brown fingernails
It's a frutti tutti monster coming for me.

## Alexander Cox (8)
St Andrew's CE (VC) Primary School, Bulmer

# The Foodlogon

Its teeth were rock sweets
And its hands were different meats.
I ran away,
But it came my way.

Its body was a cookie,
It wasn't a rookie,
I climbed up a tree,
But it was bigger than me.

Its head was a sprout,
But not a scout.
I ran,
I got a tan.

It was as big as a house,
All it did was grouse.

## Logan Pressling (9)
St Andrew's CE (VC) Primary School, Bulmer

# The Fruity Monster

Inside I hear bubbly Coke.
Mentos falling, *splash*, *splash*, *splash!*
Outside an orangey face that is very juicy.
Raisins as beady eyes.
Salt, salt, salt over me, chippy arms and legs.
I taste like toffee apples and sweeties.
I smell like fruit salad.
I am brilliant to eat.

## Amy Elizabeth Russell (8)
St Andrew's CE (VC) Primary School, Bulmer

# Chocolate Chomping Monster

He is as green as grass,
With a gigantic body,
Twelve beady eyes around his head,
Watch out when he's fed!
Chocolate is his favourite food,
But he gets in a bad mood,
Just like a volcano,
He turns red,
Stomping around
And jumping on the bed.

## Alfie Mayes-Allen (9)
St Andrew's CE (VC) Primary School, Bulmer

# The Banana Monster

As yellow as a sandy beach,
As big as the universe,
As curved as a crescent moon,
The eyes are tiny cucumbers,
It's a banana monster!

## George Griffiths (8)
St Andrew's CE (VC) Primary School, Bulmer

# Rainbow's Life

Rainbow was a friendly girl,
Who always had time to swirl and twirl,
She was a monster who always played,
And had good fun with her best friend Jade.

Although she was kind, she looked very weird,
She had a long trunk that people feared,
Coming from a country called Spain,
She preferred the sunshine and hated the rain.

Having some fun at the beach,
She holds her breath for two hours at least,
While clearing out the rubbish in the sea,
Rainbow uses her trunk so carefully.

Her and Jade's job is to keep the beach
and sea clean,
So people can come and live a summer dream,
So that is the story of Rainbow's life,
In order to help the planet and wildlife.

## Matilda Farrar (8)
St Philip's CE Primary School, Cambridge

# The Evil Snowball

Snowballs falling, soft as a doughball,
Welcome to the story of the evil snowball.
Snowballs, big ones and little ones too,
Exploding in the distance, what shall I do?
A snowball, giant adult size,
Is it just me or does that thing have eyes?
It's heading straight for me with a piercing scream,
Does it have a nose? Yes, it's blowing out steam!
A tongue shoots out from the depths of the snow,
A mouth opens wide and it knows where to go.
Wow! Look at the gleaming red eyes in the building of snow,
Its fixed stare scattering snowballs as he goes...
I'm out of breath, cheeks glowing red.
I ran and I ran, away I sped,
The snowball was close, the mouth opened wider,
I screamed and I screamed, I cried and I cried and...

I sit up in bed, where could I be?
My family peering over me.

I check my eyes aren't closed,
I wriggle my fingers, I wriggle my toes,
Yes, my feet can still move
And now it's time for me to prove,
It's just a dream, just a nightmare,
Just a dream that gave me a scare...
Night-night!

## Megan Woodward (8)
St Philip's CE Primary School, Cambridge

# Zappy And The Trouble With Lunch

Zappy was a hairy fellow,
His teeth were bared, his claws were yellow.
Famine struck Planet Xzub,
So he set off to find some grub.

Zappy came from far away,
Eating space blobs as his prey.
Monday, Tuesday, Wednesday too,
Across the galaxy he flew.

As he crashed on the grassy ground,
He stuck his head out and looked around.
He saw a granny on a stool,
His mouth began to drip and drool.

He crept up on her from the back,
Thinking she'd make a tasty snack.
He pounced upon her like a cat,
But wait a minute - what was that?

A young boy appeared around the corner
And he shouted, "I ought to warn ya,
Grannies do not taste so good,
You're better off eating healthy food.
Like broccoli, beans and peas,
Carrots and cauliflower cheese."

Zappy saw a better way,
He ate vegetables each day
And if you see him passing by,
He might be eating apple pie.

## Otis Hamilton (9)
St Philip's CE Primary School, Cambridge

# The Spotty Friend

I was looking out of my window one night
And I saw a light that was shining bright,
From the light a monster came,
He was big, fluffy and had a spotty mane,
I jumped in shock as scared as can be,
As the monster approached silently,
I ran to my bed and covered my eyes,
Because he gave me a big surprise.
As I lowered the covers from my head,
The monster came to the window and said,
"Please come out and play with me,
Don't be scared for I am friendly."
As I came out of the back door,
The monster came and he let out a
huge, happy roar.
"My name is Gizmo and I come from space,
My planet lurks near Saturn's waist."
I looked up at Gizmo and there I saw,
Not such a scary monster anymore.
We began to play games and read lots of stories,
He was so gentle and full of glory

I did not want this night to end,
As I had met such a special friend.

## Emilia Rose Bates (7)
St Philip's CE Primary School, Cambridge

# Skanky

Have you ever seen a monster called Skanky,
Whose fingers are knobbly and lanky?
If you haven't watch out, a surprise is coming,
Skanky is exceptionally cruel and cunning,
He is a blood-curdling, devious, devilish creature,
Who ate up his innocent head teacher,
With scummy green fangs and mouldy breath,
Which could cause anyone's death!
He burps louder than thunder
And his farts sound like earthquakes
And his favourite food is human cake.
He chases people down the abandoned alleyway
And it doesn't matter if it's night or day.
Take my advice and stay away from Skanky,
Remember his fingers are knobbly and lanky.

### Josh Roth (9)
St Philip's CE Primary School, Cambridge

# Hero And The Ghost

A monster called Hero, brave and bold
Loved to find mounds of precious gold
Now this Hero, he liked to eat
At dinner time he scoffed mincemeat.

One day he finished his morning munch
And was looking forward to his luscious lunch
When a ghost appeared with a colossal crunch
And ran away with Hero's brunch.

But Hero was brave
And chased it to its cave
He finally caught up with the pesky ghost
And gobbled it up like a Sunday roast.

When the Queen heard of the ghost's defeat
She decided to give Hero a golden treat
Hero took the treat back home
And spent the night on his brand-new throne!

**Finn Beardwell (8)**
St Philip's CE Primary School, Cambridge

# Toffee Apple

Fluff the monster lives on a silky soft cloud,
Above the Skittle-flavoured rainbow.
Every day she tiptoes as quiet as a kitten,
Along the cookie path,
Searching for a magnificent candy tree.
She spots a beautiful sweet-covered tree,
As tall as a giant.
There were squishy jelly babies,
Milky dairy bars and melting chocolate cake.
She jumped up like a kangeroo
And climbed the sticky honey-covered branches,
Like a spider monkey.
When she reached the very, very top,
There she found a toffee apple.
"Delicious!" she yelled. "My favourite!"

## Kiera Molloy (9)
St Philip's CE Primary School, Cambridge

# Bloodthirsty Billy

This creature, bloodthirsty and with bloody jaws
You could hear him from a mile away
Because of his roars
The king of monsters
He's laughing all day
But alas, where there are people
They all run away.

Playing with his children all day and night
Wishing he had a friend at nursery, perhaps a knight
One day he set off to find a friend
Round the corner, round a bend.

Billy found somebody who trusted him all along
She told the whole town (it didn't take long)
Now everyone in the town is nice to me
Now everyone's happy.

## Connie Cotton
St Philip's CE Primary School, Cambridge

# I Just Want A Friend

*Bling!* goes the bell for school,
Everyone quickly goes to the hall.
Suddenly the headmistress bellows,
"We've got a new monster with spots of yellow.
Now everyone get back to work
And wipe off that smirk."
"Oi, show-off, get out of the way!"
"Oh, my name's Twinkle and I feel quite grey.
Um, will you be my friend?"
"Yes, got ya - no! Just look at your trends."
A voice said, "Please will you be my buddy."
Twinkle turned around, "Of course I'll
be your buddy."

## Lilly-Rose Alderson (9)
St Philip's CE Primary School, Cambridge

# Bobster The Monster

Bobster was a monster that had a friend, Lobster,
He was going to Lobster's house when he
saw his friend,
With ice cream and a new best friend.
He went up to him and said, "Are we still going
for ice cream?"
Then Lobster said, "No, you are not my
friend anymore."
So Bobster walked away
He went back home and thought,
*I am never going to be a friend to a lobster again.*
He went to his mum's house
And said, "Can we get ice cream? I will pay."
So they both went for an ice cream.

## Ellina Russell (8)
St Philip's CE Primary School, Cambridge

# Scary Sam's Adventure

"Scary Sam, wake up, the moon's out,"
Calls Evil Eli, running about.
"Let's go and throw shining stars down
And make these earthlings grumpy and frown."

Scary Sam wakes up and grins,
He knows the fun's about to begin,
Their silver spaceship is ready to go,
Off they head to nearby Pluto.

Sam is speedy, as fast as can be,
Pinching things with four arms before
anyone can see,
With vampire bites making other monsters groan,
Scary Sam is really bad through to the bone.

## Charleigh McDonnell (9)
St Philip's CE Primary School, Cambridge

# What Is Your Monster All About?

Some monsters are kind just like mine,
They won't hurt you so you'll be fine,
Do you like something that's cute?
You know you have to watch out if they puke.

Tons of monster have their own team,
Don't you worry, my monster won't scare you in your dream.
Kiki is a very nice friend,
Don't you think that's the end.

As you can see the monsters are very kind.
Get your own monster to find.
Can't you just give it a try?
But all that's left is for monsters to cry.

## Althea Jasmaine Ladia Erum (8)
St Philip's CE Primary School, Cambridge

# The Hunt

Razorfang swims hungrily through the sea
There are lots of fish swimming quickly
Razorfang silently stalks the fish
The fish sense danger
Razorfang's pointed head breaks the surface
The fish dive down
Razorfang shoots down after his prey
The fish panic and spread out
Razorfang swims around the fish and traps them
The fish flee deeper down
Razorfang traps them at the bottom of the sea
The fish are very scared
Razorfang ensnares the fish
The fish are gone and the water is calm.

## Tom Dunne (7)
St Philip's CE Primary School, Cambridge

# A Monster Called Stomper

A monster came here from outer space,
He was alone on his planet so he came
to this place.
He was a young monster as black as the night,
He went through towns giving everyone a fright.

He could shape-shift into any type of form,
And had a growling voice like the centre
of a storm.
The poor old monster was sitting in the sun,
Watching everyone have lots of fun.

A ball came and hit him,
He was about to complain.
But instead, he asked
If he could join in the game.

## Samuel Unsworth (9)
St Philip's CE Primary School, Cambridge

# Dinko

My name is Dinko
I live in the cold
I have no friends
'Cause I can't do as I'm told

My ice cave is grand
Come visit me please
I'll try to be good
And I'll try not to sneeze

Himalayas are a cool place to live in
I'm sure you'd like it too
I am a little bit stinky
And rather hairy too

But don't be afraid
I'll do you no harm
We can make yellow snowcones
And wear them as charms.

**Mollie Brown (7)**
St Philip's CE Primary School, Cambridge

# Bob

Bob is a monster, a very happy monster,
Big and funny, like his friend Pompster,
My monster Bob is very fluffy,
Yet he is also very scruffy.

Bob is as big as an elephant and he's very hairy,
And he isn't too scary,
Bob is as fluffy as a cat,
Cylindrical but not too fat.

Bob is a lovely shade of red,
And most of all he likes his bed,
He's over the moon when he sees an owl,
As white as snow like his beach towel.

## Rhys Brown (8)
St Philip's CE Primary School, Cambridge

# Fuzzy The Monster

Fuzzy the monster is as monstrous as a bee,
No one wants him to sit on their knee,
He rips the primroses in the grass,
Everyone wants his time to pass.

There Fuzzy goes to space,
No one wants him to win the race,
He breath smells horrible,
He's really not adorable.

He's like a dragon,
But he destroys wagons,
Fuzzy's orange, fluffy but not creepy,
He's not at all sleepy.

## Anna Koscielny-Lemaire (9)
St Philip's CE Primary School, Cambridge

# The Tale Of Frightening Fiend

The monster is very scary,
He creeps me out all of the time,
In my town, he is known as the Frightening Fiend,
He is not anyone's friend.

He lives under your bed,
Sometimes you might hear a snore,
Which might sound like,
*Hoo! Shh!*

He travels around in a magic box,
Just to become your worst nightmare,
So beware of this monster,
Because you will be its next target!

## Sumayyah H Rahman (9)
St Philip's CE Primary School, Cambridge

# Once I Saw A Monster...

Once I saw a monster, with razor-sharp claws
Once I saw a monster, with feet as big as doors
This monster was not kind, it was very mean
And so hideously ugly, it didn't like being seen
But I saw it once when I was lying in my bed
It was looking through the window, eyes shining bright red
I think I saw its claw, glinting like steel
It could have been a nightmare, but it seemed very real.

## Charlotte Skates (8)
St Philip's CE Primary School, Cambridge

# Monster Day

In a meadow oh so green
Where I have seen
A monster as fast as lightning
And sometimes she sings

By the tallest tree in the world
I always see her curled
While thinking about the magic tree
She said to me, "Let's climb the tree"

So up the tree we climbed
Then the bells started to chime
Then it was time to go
But me and Lullaby have had fun you know.

**Imodgen Hodges (8)**
St Philip's CE Primary School, Cambridge

# Monster Battles

*Smoosh, whoosh,*
The battle has begun
Zap is fighting
For our fun

Steele strikes
Zap attacks
But patience
Is what Steele lacks

Steele's lost,
It retreats to the sky
Zap starts its magic
And lets out a tired sigh

Now it's all over
And it's going to be fun
Zap has brought down lots of beasts
And now has nearly done.

## Alma Dunne (9)
St Philip's CE Primary School, Cambridge

# Gobble

This is a monster called Gobble
He's horrible and scary
His hair is very messy
And his feet are very flat
His hands are wet and bumpy
He's wearing a big, white, dirty cloak
With old mud on it
He likes to roll about in it
Like a muddy bath
He looks ugly and messy
He needs to wash
Horns flowing out of his head
What a horrible monster.

## Mali Hardinge (7)
St Philip's CE Primary School, Cambridge

# Hogar The Ogre

Flash goes a strike of lightning
*Bash* go fire swords
Warriors are fighting
And so are ferocious lords

*Smack* goes Hogar's shoulder
Knocking a man out cold
*Boom* goes the boulders
As they violently roll

So Hogar jumps sky-high
Missing every single one
After taking a big sigh
He noticed he was done.

## Jay Evely (9)
St Philip's CE Primary School, Cambridge

# Hairy Five-Eyes

I live on the planet Mars which is red in colour,
I have five eyes, this means I can see the same things five times at once,
I have funny-shaped teeth, some are round, some are pointed,
I have very pretty hair, my hair is all the colours of the rainbow,
I'm very friendly but I haven't got any friends,
Would you be my friend?

## Michael Hudson (8)
St Philip's CE Primary School, Cambridge

# My Monster Friend

My friend called Mr Stinky
He only has one friend
He likes eating cheesy pizza
And never eats his friend
He is the kindest monster I have ever known
Who would hate to live all on his own
Mr Stinky is my monster
And he is my true best friend
He likes playing football every day
And I am grateful to have him as my friend.

## Corin McCarthy (8)
St Philip's CE Primary School, Cambridge

# Fluffy And Me

My monster's name is Fluffy
And he is very scruffy
Unless we go to parties
And then he gets all smarty
He may look scary
But he is a kind friend really
He is as soft as a pillow
Or even a teddy bear
He is colourful and forgetful
But full of cheer
My fluffy, forgetful friend
Makes me feel fantastic.

## Honor Day (7)
St Philip's CE Primary School, Cambridge

# Midnight

A fierce purple vision,
Is based on precision,
A nightmare to us all,
She roosts in the village hall.

Every single year,
All the good dreams disappear,
Midnight,
What a fright.

So help us please,
Get rid of this disease,
This terrible fright,
*Get lost* Midnight!

## Emily Sutton (9)
St Philip's CE Primary School, Cambridge

# Cute Luke

There was once a monster called Luke,
He was very kind, fluffy and cute,
He had a tough time at school,
Because he wasn't very scary at all!
He loved children of all ages,
He would never put them in cages!
Instead, he was considerate and kind,
He was the cutest monster you would ever find!

**Elliot Glasberg (9)**
St Philip's CE Primary School, Cambridge

# Jaws

Jaws is a very dangerous shark
And sometimes he eats people at dark
His friend Peppadile is very nice I think
And he comes from a lasagne

  **J** aws are very sharp
  **A** re very chompy
 **W** here will he go next?
  **S** omewhere in the world you will find him.

## Gideon Wilder Lynn (9)
St Philip's CE Primary School, Cambridge

# Five-Eyed Monster

It's very spotty and has five beady eyes
like a spider
Five-Eyed Beast is very silly
Loud like a lion's roar
It has big, hairy feet like a yeti
It has no friends or family
But all of the other mystical creatures
do have friends.

## Leah Davidson (10)
Waldringfield Primary School, Waldringfield

# Emperor Chicken Kenny

Emporer Chicken, his castle so tall
Emporer Chicken, his empire so small
Emporer Chicken, ruler of all
Emporer Chicken, he's not kind at all

Emporer Chicken, his name is Ken
Emporer Chicken, his mum is a hen
Emporer Chicken will raid your den

Emporer Chicken, his hobby is playing the guitar
Emporer Chicken, he travels so far
Emporer Chicken, he comes from Mars

Emporer Chicken, he claims villages from big to small
Emporer Chicken, he's very small
Emporer Chicken, he won't stop at all
Emporer Chicken, until Earth's population is one, that's all
And that one person is him
He even *killed his uncle Tim!*

## Alex Edward Clare (11)
West Walton Community Primary School, West Walton

# Sweetheart's Acrostic Poem

- **S** weetheart is soft and cuddly and she loves sweets.
- **W** here she lives is in Candy Land with her best friends.
- **E** mily is one of her friends along with Icky Gicky and Squiggles.
- **E** very day she plays with her friends in Candy Land.
- **T** he more she plays, the more friendly she becomes.
- **H** olly is the name of her owner and her house is made up of sweets.
- **E** very day Sweetheart takes a bite out of Holly's house.
- **A** lways be careful of what you eat because it could be a poisonous sweet.
- "**R** eady, set, go!" she says every time she wants to play.
- **T** o go to Rainbow Land she needs to play hopscotch for a week.

## Holly Pepper (10)
West Walton Community Primary School, West Walton

# Moon Monster

My monster is nocturnal and only seen at night,
If you wake her in the day she might give
you a fright,
My monster is very gentle,
Although she can become a bit mental.

I put her in my pocket if she wants to go for walks,
But she doesn't want to get caught so
she doesn't talk,
If she is in my pocket I will tickle her belly,
When the streets are clear she will flip
into my welly.

Now it's time to turn out the lights,
What mischief will she get up to tonight?

### Imogen Hopps (11)
West Walton Community Primary School, West Walton

# Jefferina, The Weird Monster

My monster's called Jefferina,
She's a very good ballerina,
At home she is normally asleep,
I like it because she doesn't make a peep.

Jefferina is really small,
Although her friends are really tall,
She wakes me up in the middle of the night,
It always gives me a big fright.

In the daytime she loves to sing,
After she hears the church bell ring.
You can always hear her loudly talk,
If you see her she's normally on a walk.

## Rosie Fensom (11)
West Walton Community Primary School, West Walton

# My Monster

M y monster is called Goldy
O n the forest cliffs it lives in a small tree house
N ight falls, her wings glow up
S mells of cotton candy
T he horn is shimmery and gold
E merald eyes to see in the dark
R ides in the sky with its wings and has pink fluffy fur.

## Charlotte Walker (10)
West Walton Community Primary School, West Walton

# Monster

Mighty,
Obnoxious, oblivious,
Cheeky, annoying, alien-like,
Fluffy, cute, blue-eyed, candy,
Strong, tall, candyfloss, pink,
Angel-blue, pink ears, halo,
Cuddly, funny,
Hovers.

### Chloe Puttock (10)
West Walton Community Primary School, West Walton

# YOUNG WRITERS INFORMATION

We hope you have enjoyed reading this book – and that you will continue to in the coming years.

If you're a young writer who enjoys reading and creative writing, or the parent of an enthusiastic poet or story writer, do visit our website **www.youngwriters.co.uk**. Here you will find free competitions, workshops and games, as well as recommended reads, a poetry glossary and our blog.

If you would like to order further copies of this book, or any of our other titles, then please give us a call or visit **www.youngwriters.co.uk**.

Young Writers
Remus House
Coltsfoot Drive
Peterborough
PE2 9BF
(01733) 890066
info@youngwriters.co.uk